sasol
reaching new frontiers

FIRST FIELD GUIDE TO
WILDLIFE
OF SOUTHERN AFRICA

Flap-necked Chameleon (page 20)

GW00720508

African Penguin (page 23)

SEAN FRASER AND TRACEY HAWTHORNE

Contents

Leopard (page 39)

Kudu (page 53)

Rock Monitor (page 19)

Wildlife

All forms of life can be divided into two major groups – plants, which belong to the plant kingdom, and animals – of the animal kingdom. Plants stay in one place and make their own food; animals move around and feed on other living creatures, and therefore have specially adapted

Thick-tailed Scorpion (page 12)

senses, which enable them to find what they need to eat. Animals can smell, taste, hear, see and feel.

All the animals that have backbones are known as chordates, or vertebrates. Chordates are divided into five classes, namely mammals (Mammalia), reptiles (Reptilia), amphibians (Amphibia), birds (Aves) and fish (Pisces).

Because animals like insects, spiders and scorpions have no backbones, they are known as invertebrates. They are of the order Arthropoda,and are classed as arachnids (Arachnida), and have jointed legs, which come straight out of the body.

Ecology

The many different forms of life found on Earth are all connected to one another and their environment, like links in a living chain. Every link is important: if one is lost, the whole chain is broken. Each living organism needs to feed on another, maybe smaller creature, in order to survive, and in turn is eaten by a bigger one. For example, spiders and scorpions feed on insects, as do frogs, while birds feed on arthropods and insects. Snakes eat frogs, birds and small mammals, while larger mammals, in turn, feed on the smaller mammals. Birds sometimes eat small snakes.

Southern African wildlife

The African continent is home to many different kinds of animals, and some of southern Africa's wildlife hold world records:

❧ African elephant – biggest land mammal

❧ ostrich – biggest bird

❧ giraffe – tallest mammal

❧ cheetah – fastest mammal

Chacma Baboon (page 35)

Climate and vegetation

The southern African region is made up of a wide range of vegetation types – from arid deserts and semideserts, to savanna grasslands, green woodlands and lush forests, and each of these supports its own unique species of animals.

These animals are specially adapted to survive in the climate and vegetation of the region in which they live.

Kruger National Park

There are more than 600 game parks and nature reserves in South Africa alone. The biggest of these is the Kruger National Park in the Mpumalanga and Limpopo provinces. The Kruger National Park covers nearly 20,000km^2, which means that it is bigger than some small countries. It boasts nearly 500 different species of bird, more than 100 reptile species, more than 30 types of amphibian, nearly 150 mammal species, and some 150 groups of insects.

Identifying wildlife

Spiders & Scorpions
Spiders and scorpions are spineless creatures. Both species have eight legs, and scorpions also carry a pair of pincers and a tail with a poisonous sting at the end of it. Spiders generally have eight eyes, although it is unlikely that you will get close enough to count them!

Amphibians
Amphibians lay eggs from which tadpoles are born. They develop into adults in water. Once they are fully grown, they are able to survive equally well on land and in water.

African Fish Eagle (page 27)

Snakes & other Reptiles
Tortoises, lizards, crocodiles and most snakes hatch from eggs, and have a dry, scaly skin. Unlike mammals, they are cold-blooded animals and so cannot control their body temperature; instead they heat up and cool down as the air around them does.

Birds
Birds are warm-blooded creatures and have feathers. Although all birds have wings, not all of them can fly. Birds lay eggs from which their young hatch.

Note: The common names of the birds in this book have been updated in accordance with the recommendations of an international committee.

Mammals
Mammals are warm-blooded animals with a backbone, unique jaws and teeth, and a coat of hair or fur – or, in the case of whales, 'blubber' – to help keep their bodies warm. Mammals are born alive, and are suckled by their mothers.

In order to identify a specific animal, you should study its different features, for example its **size, colour**, and **shape**; also, try to see what **food** it eats, and its surroundings or **location**. These features may tell you something about the way this animal lives, and so give you some idea of what species it is. Different animals have different **habits** and those with which you may not be familiar are marked with a ᴳ in this book. A definition of these words is given on page 56, in the Glossary.

For a realistic idea of how big an animal is – only the smaller ones, of course – use the ruler on the outside back cover. Spiders are measured from the front of the carapace ᴳ to the spinnerets ᴳ, and scorpions from the front of the head to the tip of the tail. The body length of both the Platanna and the Bullfrog is given. Only the shells of the tortoises are measured; all other reptile measurements are from the tip of the snout to the tip of the tail. The wingspan (the measurement from wingtip to wingtip) of each bird is given, or, if not available, the measurement of a single wing, i.e. from 'elbow' to wingtip, is provided. In the case of mammals, the body length is provided, as well as height to the shoulder where appropriate.

Most animals are known by a number of different names. They usually have a **common name**, which is familiar to most of us. But because the same, or similar, animals may have different names in different languages all over the world, most scientists, researchers and conservationists prefer to use the animal's **scientific name**. This is usually a Latin name, and is written in *italic* text. The ostrich's scientific name is, for example, *Struthio camelus*.

Sometimes, too, animals are given different common names by the local people of a specific region. For example, many South Africans know the ostrich by its Afrikaans **(A)** name, volstruis, its Xhosa **(X)** name, inciniba, and its Zulu **(Z)** name, intshe. (These are the most commonly spoken languages, after English, in South Africa.)

Conserving wildlife

Conservation means protecting and managing the natural environment – the land and all the living things on, below and above it.

Many kinds of animals and plants have become extinct since life first began on Earth. Although a large number of them disappeared before the arrival of human beings, modern man has played a major role in the destruction of Nature over the past few thousand years.

More than 200 birds and mammals have become extinct in the past 2,000 years alone.

Humans hunt wild animals; they build bigger cities to house their growing numbers; they mine metals and minerals from the ground; and they cultivate millions of hectares of farm land to fill billions of empty stomachs. In the process, wild animals are robbed of their natural environment and left to survive on small pieces of land.

Learning about wild animals may help us to understand the role they play in our lives and how the Earth will suffer if they are lost forever.

About five per cent of the world's mammals and nearly eight per cent of birds are found in South Africa. This wonderful diversity of animals not only makes southern Africa one of the richest wildlife regions in the world, but also places a responsibility on all of us to conserve our unique environment for future generations.

Wild Dogs (page 41)

In the field

Be responsible

* Do not litter.
* Put out cooking fires.
* Never harm or interfere with wild animals.
* Wild animals should never be removed from their natural habitat.

Danger in the bush

* Never leave your car, unless a sign says you may.
* Never feed or try to pet wild animals.
* Some birds, for example the crowned lapwing, will attack viciously if you go near its nest.

Giraffe (page 49)

* Elephant cows are fiercely protective of calves, and will charge and attack when they feel that their young are being threatened.
* Hippos move along fixed paths on river banks during sunrise and sunset. Do not cross these paths – there's an old saying: 'Never stand between a hippopotamus and the water'! If caught off guard, a frightened hippo may attack a human being.
* Almost all spiders and scorpions are venomous, but few spiders are dangerous to humans. All scorpions, however, deliver painful stings – and some can even kill you.

Garden Orb-web Spiders

Argiope

Family Araneidae, subfamily Argiopinae.

African names:
Tuinwawielwebspinnekoppe (A).

Average size: Length: 25mm (f); leg span up to 80mm.

Identification: Females usually large and spectacular, silver and yellow with black markings, sometimes with ribbed or lobed abdomen[G]. Long, banded legs. Males usually small and plain.

Where found: Bushy countryside where they can spin webs between trees and tall shrubs. In built-up areas in trees, bushes, plants, grass and other low-growing vegetation.

Habits: Diurnal[G]. Moves about very little; web-bound. Female hangs upside down in web, with two pairs each of back and front legs held together. Spider wraps captured prey in silk, then bites and kills victim; sometimes leaves prey hanging until it is hungry. Spins huge, wheel-like orb web, up to 75cm across.

Notes: Larger specimens can inflict painful bite but none are known to be venomous.

Status: Common.

Food: Insects.

Reproduction: Tiny male waits until female has captured prey and is feeding, then mates with her while she is distracted. Female spins egg sac, camouflaged according to environment.

Similar species: Grass Orb-web Spider.

Black Button Spider

Latrodectus indistinctus

Family Theridiidae.

African names: Swartknopie-spinnekop (A); isigcawu esiliqhosha elimnyama (X); isicabucabu esinechashazi elimnyama (Z).

Average size: Length: 15mm (f); 3.5mm (m); leg span up to 40mm.

Identification: Black, globular abdomen^G with dull red dot or stripe on upper surface. Long legs, third pair shortest. Comb-like 'bristles' on fourth leg. Male brown, smaller than female.

Where found: In trees; under stones, bushes, grass, leaf litter, rotting logs in forests.

Habits: Nocturnal^G. Moves about very little; web-bound. Male usually found along border of female's web. Uses 'bristles' on fourth leg to fling sticky silk over prey, then delivers fatal bite. Shams death when threatened.

Reproduction: Makes smooth, round, pea-sized egg sacs.

Notes: Sometimes known as 'black widow spider' for its habit of eating male after mating.

Status: Common.

Venom: Potent neurotoxin^G, causing nausea, vomiting, cramping pains in chest and joints, fever, sweating and difficulty in breathing; potentially lethal to humans, especially children.

Food: Insects (beetles); small vertebrates.

Similar species: Black-phase Brown Button Spider; False Button Spider.

Thick-tailed Scorpions

Parabuthus

Family Buthidae.

African names:
Dikstertskerpioene (A); unomadudwane omsila utyebileyo (X); ufezela onomsila omkhulu (Z).

Average size: Length: 9cm.

Identification: Yellow, olive-yellow or yellow-brown to dark brown and almost black. Thin pincers; thick tail. Ridges on upper surface of first two tail segments.

Where found: Under stones, in burrows, under dried cowpats, near houses and outbuildings.

Habits: May squirt venom into the eyes. When threatened, stridulates (makes a harsh noise) by scraping stinger across peg-like granules on tail.

Notes: The most serious stings in the region can be attributed to scorpions of this family.

Status: Common.

Venom: Potently neurotoxic[G] and potentially lethal.

Food: Insects, including cockroaches and termites.

Reproduction: Depending on the species, gestation is between a few and 18 months. Most scorpions give birth to live young. Younglings generally stay with the mother until the first moult.

Similar species: Bark Scorpions.

Common Platanna

Xenopus laevis

African names: Gewone platanna (A); iplatana elijwayelekile (X); unoplatana oqhelekileyo (Z)

Average size: 7.5cm.

Identification: Oval-shaped body with slimy, mottled grey skin. Tiny arms with small, feeble fingers. Large, webbed hindfeet with clawed toes.

Where found: Water.

Habits: Very good swimmer; mostly found underwater. Large numbers may travel overland in search of better habitats. Produces a soft, buzzing call.

Notes: The closely related Cape platanna (*Xenopus gilli*) is endangered, because vleis and other water sources in which it lives have either been drained or are badly polluted.

Status: Common.

Food: Mostly insects.

Reproduction: Fish-like tadpoles hatch from small black eggs laid on stones or plants under the water. Tadpole takes four to five weeks to reach adulthood. This process is known as metamorphosis.

Similar species: Cape Platanna.

Giant Bullfrog

Pyxicephalus adspersus

Habits: Its name is derived from its deep, bellowing call, which resembles that of a young bull; also brays loudly when in danger.

Notes: Young are bright green in colour, with black stippling and a pale stripe running down the centre of the back. Unlike most other frogs, the male is bigger than the female.

African names: Grootbrulpadda (A); ingxangxa (X); indubule (Z).

Average size: 20cm.

Identification: The giant bullfrog is a huge, olive-green frog with ridges on its skin. Undersides are yellow, and armpits are orange-yellow. The African bullfrog (Pyxicephalus edulis) has a darker, brownish-green back covered with dark spots.

Where found: Pans.

Status: Near threatened.

Food: Small birds, rodents, other frogs.

Reproduction: Eggs are laid in shallow water and tadpoles take four to five weeks to metamorphose, or develop into adults.

Similar species: African bullfrog.

Leopard Tortoise

Stigmochelys pardalis

African names: Bergskilpad (A); ufudo olubuhlosi (X); ufudu lwengwe (Z)

Average size: Length 37cm (up to 70cm in E. Cape); weight 10kg (up to 40kg in E. Cape).

Identification: Dome-shaped shell with slightly raised plates. Shells of young are yellow with single black spots marking the plates. Spots spread and streak with age. Adults are generally a dark greyish brown.

Where found: Montane grassland, bushveld, savanna, fynbos.

Habits: Shelters in dense, bushy areas during cold weather.

Notes: Grows very slowly; weighs only about 1kg at eight years.

Status: Locally common.

Food: Plants, but also gnaws on hyaena faeces and bones to obtain calcium for shell growth.

Reproduction: Lays five to 15 eggs; 12-month incubation[G]; at birth young measure 4–5cm and weigh 45g each.

Similar species: Geometric Tortoise.

Leatherback Sea Turtle

Dermochelys coriacea

African names: Leerrugskilpad (A); ufudo lwaselwandle i-leatherback (X); ufudu lwasolwande oluneqolo elisasikhumba (Z).

Average size: Length 1.5m; weight up to 800kg.

Identification: It has a black head and carapace^G, spotted with pale grey or blue. The carapace^G is rubbery, and has 12 prominent ridges. The head has a pink or reddish mark on top. Underparts are black, white and pink. The tail is black. Long flippers.

Notes: The heaviest living reptile.

Status: Endangered.

Food: Jellyfish.

Reproduction: Breeds on Maputaland beaches. Female lays six to nine clutches, each containing up to 120 white, billiard ball-sized eggs. Hatchlings emerge about 10 weeks later. Growth rate is rapid: reaches adult size in 3–5 years.

Similar species: Loggerhead Sea Turtle.

Where found: Tropical to temperate oceans (marine); beaches when laying eggs.

Habits: Lacks teeth; horny spines in throat enable it to swallow slippery prey.

Southern African Python

Python natalensis

African names: Suider-Afrikaanse luislang, rotsluislang (A); inamba, ugqoloma (X); inhlwathi yase-Afrika eseningizimu (Z).

Average size: Length 3–4m.

Identification: Thick, greyish-brown body covered with small, smooth scales; dark stripes and blotches on upper half of body; lighter underparts with dark spots.

Where found: Rocky areas in arid terrain, and in moist savanna, often near water (especially riverine scrub). Absent only from true desert and dense rainforest.

Habits: Favours rocky outcrops. Often found basking in the sun. More active at night, when it is guided to its warm-blooded prey by heat receptors situated on the upper lip (these enable it to strike accurately in the dark).

Notes: Largest snake in Africa; uses its long body to suffocate its prey.

Status: Vulnerable.

Food: Mostly small rodents, dassies, monkeys, ground-living birds, and small antelope.

Reproduction: Lays 30 to 60 eggs; three-month incubation[G]; young measure 50–70cm at birth.

Cape Cobra

Naja nivea

African names: Kaapse Kobra, Koperkapel, Geelslang (A); umdlambila (X); imfezi yakwelaseKapa (Z).

Average size: Length 1.3m.

Identification: Slender with broad head and dull scales. Colours vary from yellow (goldish, sometimes speckled with brown), brown (red-brown, or mahogany), to black.

Where found: Mostly dry regions, particularly dry river courses.

Habits: Usually nocturnal[G], but has been known to hunt by day. Primarily terrestrial[G], but will climb low-growing trees.

Notes: Raises its head and spreads a hood while advancing on victim, but does not spit. Venom is paralysing and deadly.

Status: Common; endemic[G].

Food: Birds' eggs, other snakes, rodents, lizards and toads.

Reproduction: Lays eight to 20 eggs. Young (measuring 30–40cm) born after a three-month incubation[G] period.

Similar species: Mole Snake.

Southern Rock/White-throated Monitor

Varanus albigularis

African names: Veldlikkewaan (A); i-rock monitor (X); uxamu wase-madwaleni (Z).

Average size: Length 1.75m (incl. tail, which is longer than body).

Identification: A large lizard with well-developed limbs, strong claws and a long tail. The skin is tough and covered with bead-like scales at midbody. The back is dark greyish brown, with a few blotches of yellow. The belly is a dirty yellow. Banded tail.

Where found: Savanna and dry, semidesert areas.

Habits: Hibernates (entering an inactive, sleep-like state) during winter. If attacked, it bites readily, and lashes with its tail.

Notes: Only lizard with a forked tongue. Sheds skin.

Status: Common.

Food: Mostly millipedes, beetles, grasshoppers, snails, but also a variety of other small animals.

Reproduction: Lays eight to 51 eggs; four-month incubation^G. Young (25cm long) weigh 19g.

Similar species: Nile Monitor.

Common Flap-neck Chameleon

Chamaeleo dilepis

African names: Flapnekverkleurmannetjie (A); ulovane olunentamo esixwexwe (X); unwabu olunentamo ebhakuzayo (Z).

Average size: Length 15cm (incl. tail, which is same length as body).

Identification: A large chameleon with a continuous crest of tubercles (small, rounded growths) along the throat and belly, and flaps at the back of the skull. Body colour varies from light yellow to green, sometimes brown.

Notes: Tongue is sticky, moist and soft; as it shoots out, the end wraps around prey, sucking onto it. When alarmed, raises flaps and opens mouth wide to show threatening orange lining.

Status: Common.

Food: Insects, spiders, snails, centipedes.

Reproduction: Lays 25 to 55 eggs; five-month incubation[G]. Hatchlings are 5cm long.

Similar species: Namaqua Chameleon.

Where found: Savanna woodland and coastal forest areas in northern, central and eastern regions.

Habits: Primarily arboreal[G]. Changes colour for camouflage (disguise to escape notice of predators[G]).

Nile Crocodile

Crocodylus niloticus

African names: Nylkrokodil (A); ingwenya yomNayile (X); ingwenya yaseNile (Z).

Average size: Length 3m (tail makes up 40% of length); weight up to 1,000kg.

Identification: An ancient-looking reptile with a long jaw, prominent teeth, and a long tail. Horny plates cover the body, and the ones on top of the head are fused to the skull. Eyes and nostrils are situated on top of the head.

Where found: Swamps and backwaters, larger rivers, lakes, river mouths.

Habits: Baby crocodiles produce a high-pitched noise before hatching, calling the mother to open the nest.

Notes: Adults attack game at water's edge, dragging them into the water and drowning them.

Status: Vulnerable.

Food: Buck, zebra, buffalo and even humans. Also fish, birds.

Reproduction: Lays 16 to 80 eggs in a hole. Hatchlings (25–32cm) appear after three months.

Ostrich

Struthio camelus

African names: Volstruis (A); inciniba (X); intshe (Z).

Average size: Male up to 2m.

Identification: Unmistakable bird; small head, long neck. Male has black body feathers, white wingtips, chestnut-coloured tail and long legs. Female greyish brown.

Where found: Virtually throughout the region.

Habits: Usually in small groups, but young birds may gather in large flocks. Young can run at up to 60km/hour (at one month old) – with wings outstretched to balance the body.

Notes: Largest bird in the world. Cannot fly. Can be very dangerous when threatened and is known to kick assailants. Wild ostriches are found in many areas, while others in the region are descendants of birds that were bred for their feathers.

Status: Locally common.

Food: Grass, berries, seeds, plants, reptiles, and insects.

Nesting: Lays three to eight eggs; the incubation[G] period is 39 to 53 days.

African Penguin

Spheniscus demersus

African names: Bril-pikkewyn (A); iphengwini (X); inguza (Z).

Average size: Length 60cm; length of flipper 16.5cm.

Identification: Upperparts black; underparts white. Face black-and-white with pink eyebrow, and thick, black bill. A black band extends from the leg, up the side of the body, over the upper chest, down to the other leg – forming almost a complete circle.

Where found: Along the coast and on offshore islands.

Habits: Brays like a donkey. It also growls during fights.

Notes: The juvenile[G] bird lacks bold patterning and is greyish blue in colour, with a white front and no black markings.

Status: Vulnerable; endemic[G].

Food: Anchovies, gobies, squid, and octopus.

Nesting: Lays two eggs; 36-day incubation[G].

White Stork

Ciconia ciconia

African names: Witooievaar (A); ingwamza, unowanga (X); unogolantethe, unowanga (Z).

Average size: Length 1m; wingspan 1.6m.

Identification: White all over, apart from black flight feathers. Bill, legs and feet are red. Thin, long bill and legs.

Where found: Vleis, grassland, cultivated land.

Habits: Usually in flocks. Migratory[G] bird; breeds in northern hemisphere. Stabs at prey with long bill while foraging. Roosts (rests or sleeps) in trees. Makes no call, but claps its bill.

Notes: In very hot weather it deposits its droppings on its legs to lower its body temperature.

Status: Common.

Food: Locusts and other large insects, small reptiles, mammals, frogs, tadpoles, molluscs.

Nesting: Lays three eggs; 34-day incubation[G].

Similar species: Black Stork.

Egyptian Goose

Alopochen aegyptiaca

African names: Kolgans (A); ilowe (X); ilongwe (Z).

Average size: Length 68cm; wing 38cm.

Identification: Mainly buff-brown above. Dark brown eye mask; dark brown patch on centre of breast. Metallic green secondaries^G. In flight shows conspicuous white forewings. Juvenile^G is duller, developing brown mask and breast patch after 3–5 months.

Where found: Throughout the region, except in deserts. Occurs on inland waters, estuaries and coastal lakes, and in cultivated fields.

Habits: Gregarious^G when not breeding, otherwise in pairs. Wary, quickly flies off when approached. Male hisses. Both sexes honk repeatedly with neck out-stretched when alarmed or taking flight.

Notes: This bird is valued as a game bird. Can become an agricultural pest.

Status: Very common resident.

Food: Grass, leaves, seeds, grain, aquatic rhizomes and tubers.

Nesting: Monogamous^G. Breeds all year round, but mainly in spring. Lays five to 11 cream-coloured eggs, which hatch after about a month. Female incubates^G; both parents feed young.

Similar species: South African Shelduck.

White-backed Vulture

Gyps africanus

African name: Witrugaasvoël (A).

Average size: Length 94cm; wingspan 2.2m.

Identification: Large. Generally streaky brown. Blackish face and neck. White lower back in flight. Dark eyes.

Where found: Northern half of the region, in savanna and bushveld.

Habits: Gregarious^G. Roosts^G in trees at night; often rests on ground during day. Drinks and bathes regularly at water holes. Makes goose-like hisses, and cackles and squeals; also grunts.

Notes: The most common vulture in southern Africa, and the most frequently seen in bushveld game reserves.

Status: Locally common resident.

Food: Carrion, bone fragments.

Nesting: In winter. Builds platform of sticks high in a tree; may use nest for a few years. One white egg is laid. Both sexes incubate^G; egg hatches after about two months. Both sexes feed young.

Similar species: Cape Vulture.

African Fish Eagle

Haliaeetus vocifer

African names: Visarend (A); unomakh-wezana (X); inkwazi (Z).

Average size: Length 68cm; wingspan 1.9m (m), 2.3m (f).

Identification: Unmistakable, with white head and 'bib', black back and wings, chestnut underparts and short, white tail. Yellow cere (swelling at the base of the upper beak) and legs, black beak.

Where found: Rivers, lakes, dams, estuaries and lagoons.

Habits: Usually found in pairs. Call is loud and shrill, and often in duet. Swoops down over the water and catches fish with feet.

Notes: One of the best-known birds of prey in the world; its call, an unmistakeable 'kyow-kyow-kow', is one of the most familiar sounds of Africa.

Status: Locally common.

Food: Mainly fish, also carrion, eggs; sometimes small mammals (dassies, monkeys), frogs, leguaans.

Nesting: Usually lays two eggs; about 45-day incubation[G].

Similar species: Palm-nut Vulture.

Black-shouldered Kite

Elanus caeruleus

African names: Blouvalk (A); umdlampuku, unongwevana (X).

Average size: Length 33cm; wingspan 74cm.

Identification: Pale grey above, white below. Diagnostic^G black shoulder patches. Black bill with yellow cere (at base of upper beak); yellow feet; red eyes.

Where found: Virtually throughout, in varied habitats (agricultural areas; also grassland, woodland, savanna, semiarid scrub).

Habits: Solitary or in pairs by day; roosts (rests or sleeps) communally at night. Hunts from perch or by hovering over prey. Call is a wheezy 'peeu'; also whistles and screams, and makes soft 'weeep-weeep' noises.

Notes: Very common; often seen perched on telephone poles.

Status: Common resident with local movements.

Food: Mainly rodents; also small birds, reptiles and insects.

Nesting: Year round, mainly in rainy season; may breed several times a year. Both sexes build a small stick platform in which two to six eggs are laid. Incubation^G, mostly by female, takes a month.

Similar species: Lizard Buzzard.

Helmeted Guineafowl

Numida meleagris

African names: Gewone tarentaal (A); impangele (X); impangele (Z).

Average size: Length 55cm; wing 26.5cm.

Identification: Slate-grey body, finely spotted with white. Small, naked, blue-and-red head. Prominent 'helmet'.

Where found: Virtually throughout, in grassland, vleis, savanna, cultivated lands, bushveld.

Habits: Gregarious[G]; flocks may number in hundreds. Roosts (rests or sleeps) communally in trees at night. Makes a grating 'cherrrrr' sound, or gives staccato 'kek-kek-kek' alarm call; also whistles.

Notes: More than one female may lay eggs in the same nest, producing a combined clutch of up to 50 eggs.

Status: Common resident.

Food: Seeds, bulbs, tubers, berries, insects, snails, and ticks.

Nesting: Mainly in summer, in long grass or under bush. Six to 19 light yellowish-brown eggs are laid. They hatch after about a month. Only the female incubates[G].

Similar species: Crested Guineafowl.

Blue Crane

Anthropoides paradiseus

African names: Bloukraanvoël (A); indwe (X); indwa (Z).

Average size: Length 1m; wing 55cm.

Identification: Long legs and long, thin neck; long feathers like tail streamers. Blue-grey in colour, with white crown. Legs and feet are black. Recognised in flight by its outstretched neck.

Where found: Vleis, marshes, grassland, Karoo scrub, farmlands.

Habits: Usually found in small groups, sometimes in large flocks, but pair off during the breeding season. During this time, it engages in courtship dancing in which it bows, leaps in the air, takes short runs and tosses up bits of grass.

Notes: South Africa's national bird.

Status: Fairly common resident; endemic[G].

Food: Green shoots, grain, frogs, reptiles, insects, fish.

Nesting: Two eggs; one-month incubation[G].

Similar species: Wattled Crane.

Crowned Lapwing (Plover)

Vanellus coronatus

African names: Kroonkiewiet (A); igxiya (X); ititihoye (Z).

Average size: Length 30cm; wing 20cm.

Identification: Mainly greyish brown; dark band separating brown breast from white belly. Black crown, ringed with white 'halo'; black forehead. Long, red legs.

Where found: Virtually throughout, in short grasslands and other lawn-like habitats.

Habits: Gregarious^G when not breeding. Often active at night. Makes a very noisy, strident 'kreeep' sound.

Notes: Quick to react to disturbance, they will 'scream' at intruders; birds with young or hatching eggs will noisily 'divebomb' intruders to the area.

Status: Common resident.

Food: Arthropods.

Nesting: Mostly in spring. Two to four well-marked, dark olive-brown eggs are laid in a shallow scrape in the ground. Both sexes incubate^G; eggs hatch after about a month.

Western Barn Owl

Tyto alba

African names: Nonnetjie-uil (A); isikhova (X); isikhova, umzwelele (Z).

Average size: Length 30–34cm; wing 24–30cm.

Identification: Distinct white, heart-shaped face with small, black eyes. Head, back and wings are light grey and tawny; chest and underparts are off-white.

Where found: Trees, caves, old buildings, moist savanna and woodlands.

Habits: Usually in pairs. Hunts at night and roosts (rests or sleeps) during the day. Does not hoot like other owls; call ranges from snores to drawn-out shrieks.

Notes: Found almost worldwide.

Status: Common.

Food: Rodents, small birds, lizards, insects.

Nesting: Lays five eggs; one-month incubation[G].

Similar species: African Grass Owl.

Common Fiscal

Lanius collaris

African names: Fiskaallaksman (A); inxanxadi, umxhomi (X); ilunga, iqola (Z).

Average size: Length 22cm; wing 9cm.

Identification: Black above, white below; at rest shows bold white 'V' on back. Longish, white-edged black tail. Heavy, black, hooked bill.

Where found: Virtually throughout, except in forest and desert.

Habits: Territorial[G]. Perches conspicuously. May be very aggressive towards other birds. Makes piping and grating noises; also imitates other birds.

Notes: Often seen in gardens, where it chases off other bird species. Known as 'Jackie Hangman' for its habit of impaling uneaten prey on thorns or spikes.

Status: Common resident.

Food: Insects, small lizards, frogs and birds.

Nesting: Year round; may raise several broods per season. Female builds thick-walled bowl in tree, in which up to five eggs are laid; these hatch after about two weeks. Both sexes feed chicks.

Similar species: Fiscal Flycatcher.

House Sparrow

Passer domesticus

African names: Huismossie (A).

Average size: Length 14cm; wing 7cm.

Identification: Brown above, with grey rump. Male has grey cap, reddish-brown back, white cheeks and black throat. Female is duller grey-brown and has off-white eye stripe.

Where found: Throughout, always around human habitation.

Habits: In pairs or family groups when breeding, otherwise gregarious^G, sometimes in flocks of hundreds. Hops about on ground; sometimes catches flying insects on the move. Makes sharp, harsh, penetrating chirps and cheeps.

Notes: Most cosmopolitan bird in the world.

Status: Common to abundant resident.

Food: Seeds, buds, fruit, insects, spiders, household scraps.

Nesting: Year round, mainly in spring and summer. Nest is untidy. Lays two to five eggs which hatch after about two weeks. Both sexes incubate^G and feed young.

Similar species: Cape Sparrow, Great Sparrow.

Chacma Baboon

Papio ursinus

African names: Bobbejaan (A); imfene (X, Z).

Average size: Length 1.4m (m), 1.1m (f); weight 32kg (m), 15kg (f).

Identification: Body is relatively large; covered with grey to grey-brown hair. Long, pointed snout. First part of tail is held erect, but rest hangs straight down. Male has powerful shoulders, with a mane around the neck, and a single patch of bare skin under the tail. The female has one bare patch on each buttock.

Where found: Throughout the region in almost any environment, except in very dry parts.

Habits: Terrestrial[G], but also an excellent climber. Gregarious[G]; troops of 15, or even 100, led by a dominant male. Diurnal[G].

Notes: May try to scavenge from cars.

Status: Common.

Food: Omnivorous[G], but mostly fruit, leaves, seeds, grass, roots.

Reproduction: Six-month gestation[G]; single young weighing 800g.

Similar species: Yellow Baboon.

Southern African Ground Squirrel

Xerus inauris

African names: Grondeekhoring (A); unomatse wasemhlabeni (X); ingwejeje yaphansi (Z).

Average size: Length 55cm; weight 750g.

Identification: Small, with short, prickly body hair. Usually greyish brown in colour with a fainter stripe down each side of the body. Small, pointed face and tiny ears. Long, fluffy tail with black and white markings.

Where found: Dry, open areas with little vegetation.

Habits: Highly gregarious^G; large groups of between four and 30 with several dominant females. Diurnal^G; may use bushy tail to shade body from sun. Digs very long burrows^G in which it sleeps. Burrows are often shared with yellow mongooses and suricates. Terrestrial^G.

Notes: Always on the lookout for predators^G; gives a loud whistle when it senses danger.

Status: Common.

Food: Mostly vegetarian. Diet includes roots, bulbs, grass, pods, and seeds.

Reproduction: One-and-a-half-month gestation^G; two or three young weighing 20g each.

Similar species: Yellow Mongoose.

Spotted Hyaena

Crocuta crocuta

African names: Gevlekte hiëna (A); ingcuka enamacho- koza (X); impisi enamachashaza (Z).

Average size: Length 1.5m; height 80cm; weight 70kg.

Identification: High shoulders, sloping back, low rump; yellow-brown coat covered with dark splotches; mane-like patch of hair around neck. Big head with large, rounded ears. Short, hairy tail.

Where found: Open plains, woodland savanna and dry areas.

Habits: Usually lives in family groups known as clans, in which females are dominant. Territorial^G. Marks territories with droppings and secretions from anal glands. Nocturnal^G.

Expert hunter.

Notes: Makes human-like chuckling sounds; also shrieks and growls. Its loud 'whoop' call is characteristic of the African night.

Status: Common in protected areas only.

Food: Hunts antelope and zebra, but may also scavenge.

Reproduction: Three-and-a-half-month gestation^G; litter of one to two cubs weighing 1.5kg each.

Similar species: Brown Hyaena.

Cheetah

Acinonyx jubatus

African names: Jagluiperd (A); ingwenkala (X); ingulule (Z).

Average size: Length 2m; height 1m; weight 50kg.

Identification: The lean body and long legs are pale and covered with black spots from the head to the tail. Black stripes, or 'tears', run down the sides of the face, from the inner eye to the outer corner of the mouth.

Where found: Open spaces and areas with few trees.

Habits: Females live alone with their cubs. Males live alone or in groups of two or three. Hunts during the cooler times of the day by stalking its victim and then making a quick dash for the kill.

Notes: Fastest land animal in the world, reaching about 100km per hour over short distances.

Status: Locally common.

Food: Feeds on birds, and small and medium-sized antelope.

Reproduction: Three-month gestation^G; litter of three cubs weighing 300g each.

Similar species: Leopard.

Leopard

Panthera pardus

African names: Luiperd (A); ihlosi (X); ingwe (Z).

Average size: Length 1.9m; height 80cm; weight 80kg (m), 50kg (f).

Identification: Big and strong; powerful jaws. Body is light-coloured and covered with small rosettes[G]. Legs, head and rump are covered with black spots; belly is white. Long, rosette-covered tail is white underneath.

Where found: Able to live almost anywhere.

Habits: Solitary and territorial[G]; marks territory with droppings and urine. Nocturnal[G]. Hunts by stalking, and then leaping out onto prey.

Notes: Well camouflaged in trees and tall grasses.

Status: Locally common.

Food: Diet consists of birds, antelope, dassies – and even rats and mice.

Reproduction: Three-and-a-half-month gestation[G]; one to three cubs weighing 500g each.

Similar species: Cheetah.

Lion

Panthera leo

African names: Leeu (A); ingonyama (X); ibhubesi (Z).

Average size: Length 3m (m), 2.5m (f); height 1.5m (m), 1.2m (f); weight 200kg (m), 140kg (f).

Identification: Largest African predator^G; light brown to brownish red in colour; long tail ends in a dark tuft of hair. Male has bushy mane around the head and throat.

Where found: Able to live in almost any habitat.

Habits: Lives in prides of usually two or three males, and several females and their offspring. Females hunt together in groups.

Notes: Lionesses do the hunting, usually at night or towards nightfall, by ambushing prey; males eat first.

Status: Vulnerable.

Food: Hunts most large and small mammals, including antelope.

Repro-duction: Three-and-a-half-month gestation^G period; one to four cubs weighing 1.5kg each.

African Wild Dog

Lycaon pictus

African names: Wildehond (A); inja yasendle (X, Z).

Average size: Length 1.3m; height 80cm; weight 25kg.

Identification: Patches of yellow, white, black and brown hair cover the thin body and long, slender legs. Face is pale, but mouth area is dark; ears are round. Tufted tail is mostly white.

Where found: Savanna woodlands and hilly country; also open plains and areas with short grass and little vegetation.

Habits: Lives in packs of about 12; hunt together during early morning or late afternoon.

Relentlessly pursues prey; seldom gives up until it has made a kill. Only kills to eat. There is only one breeding pair per pack.

Notes: One of Africa's most endangered mammals.

Status: Endangered.

Food: Impala and other small antelope.

Reproduction: Two-and-a-half-month gestation^G; litter of seven to 12 pups, weighing 300g each.

Black-backed Jackal

Canis mesomelas

African names: Swartrugjakkals (A); udyakalashe onomqolo omnyama (X); impungushe emhlane omnyama (Z).

Average size: Length 1m; height 45cm; weight 8kg.

Identification: Reddish in colour with broad stripe of silvery black along back; black tail. Sharp, pointed ears with tufts of white hair inside. Areas around the lower mouth, under the neck and on the chest are almost white.

Where found: Prefers dry areas, but found almost throughout region.

Habits: Usually lives alone, in pairs or in small family packs. Nocturnal[G].

Notes: Known to be very clever, and constantly on the lookout for danger.

Wails towards nightfall; also yaps.

Status: Common.

Food: Mice, rabbits, birds, snakes, lizards and fruit, and even small buck; also carrion.

Reproduction: Two-month gestation[G]; litter of one to six pups weighing 380g each.

Similar species: Side-striped Jackal.

African Elephant

Loxodonta africana

African names: Olifant (A); indlovu (X, Z).

Average size: Height 3.4m (m), 2.5m (f); weight 6,000kg (m), 3,500kg (f).

Identification: Grey-brown in colour, with a thick, leathery skin. Trunk 1.5m long; big ears, ivory tusks.

Where found: Dry savanna and woodland. Needs plenty of food and water.

Habits: Small family groups of mothers and calves led by an old cow. Bulls live separately in small groups.

Notes: World's largest land mammal. Usually not dangerous, but will charge if wounded or when protecting calves.

Status: Common.

Food: Eats about 300kg of plants, fruits, leaves and grass, and drinks about 200 litres of water in a day.

Reproduction: 22-month gestation^G; single calf weighing 120kg. Only breeds every three to four years.

Rock Hyrax (Dassie)

Procavia capensis

African names: Klipdassie (A); imbila (X, Z).

Average size: Length 50cm; height 30cm; weight 3.5kg.

Identification: Small, stocky body covered with light to dark brown hair; no tail. Sharply pointed face; small, rounded ears. Short legs; glands on feet secrete moisture, enabling it to grip rock surfaces.

Where found: Rocky, mountainous terrain.

Habits: Lives in groups of up to 17 females together with their young, with a single, dominant male. Diurnal[G], but may feed at night.

Notes: One adult keeps guard while the others feed or lie in the sun. It gives a whooping warning call when it sees or hears danger, so that the group can take cover among rocks or in cracks in the rock faces. Considered by some scientists to be the closest living relative to the elephant.

Status: Common.

Food: Leaves, fruit and grass.

Reproduction: Seven-month gestation[G]; two or three young weighing 200g each.

Similar species: Tree Dassie, Yellow-spotted Rock Dassie.

White Rhinoceros

Ceratotherium simum

Vulnerable to poaching: population distribution confidential.

African names: Witrenoster (A); umkhombe omhlope (X); ubhejane, omhlophe (Z).

Average size: Height 1.8m; weight 1,800kg.

Identification: Lips are square-shaped. Has two horns, and big, pointed ears. Prominent hump on the back of the neck.

Where found: Areas with lots of short grass, shady bushes and fresh water.

Habits: Lives in groups of three or four; males territorial^G. Poor eyesight, but quick to respond to dangerous sounds or smells.

Notes: The white rhino's broad, square-shaped muzzle is adapted to feeding on grasses – hence the alternative common name of 'square-lipped rhino'.

Status: Near threatened.

Food: Grazer^G; feeds on short grasses and low-growing plants.

Reproduction: 16-month gestation^G; single calf of 40kg.

Similar species: Black rhinoceros.

Plains Zebra

Equus quagga

African names: Vlaktesebra (A); iqwarha elisitywakadi (X); idube lasethafeni (Z).

Average size: Height 1.3m; weight 300kg.

Identification: Black-and-white striped coat; shadow stripes superimposed on white stripes, especially on the rump Long mane of black-and-white hair extends from top of head to shoulders.

Where found: Open grassland and savanna plains.

Habits: Lives in small family groups, but may also be seen grazing[G] with antelope such as wildebeest.

Notes: Young males may form bachelor[G] herds. Stallions are fiercely protective of their mares.

Status: Common in protected areas.

Food: Grazes[G] on grasses, but may also browse[G] on leaves and shoots.

Reproduction: 12-month gestation[G]; a single foal weighing 30kg.

Similar species: Cape Mountain Zebra.

Warthog

Phacochoerus africanus

African names:
Vlakvark (A);
inxagu (X);
intibane (Z).

Average size: Height 70cm (m),
60cm (f); weight 80kg (m),
60kg (f).

Identification: Powerful body
and pig-like face with long
snout. Pronounced bumps
('warts') above nostrils and on
either side of eyes. Grey skin
covered with scattered bristly
hair. Long-haired mane; very
thin tail ending in clump of hair.
Adults have curved
tusks, and whisker-like
hairs on the face.

Where found: Prefers
wide, open woodlands.

Habits: Family groups
(called 'sounders')
generally consist of
a mother and her
litter, and sometimes
a boar; boars usually
live in bachelor^G herds.
Diurnal^G.

Notes: Tail is held

upright when running. Kneels
on front legs when feeding.
Uses tusks (two pairs), which
are actually canine teeth,
as weapons.

Status: Common.

Food: Mostly grazers^G, feeding
on grass and plant roots.

Reproduction: Six-month
gestation^G; two or three piglets
weighing 600g each.

Similar species:
Bushpig.

Hippopotamus

Hippopotamus amphibius

African names: Seekoei (A); imvubu (X, Z).

Average size: Height 1.5m; weight 1,500kg.

Identification: Huge body covered in smooth, dark grey skin. Massive, powerful jaws; huge canine and incisor teeth. Short legs, with four toes on each foot.

Where found: Rivers, lakes and lagoons.

Habits: Lives in groups of about 12 cows and calves, headed by a bull. Roams river banks at night in search of food. Bulls mark their territory by spreading their dung; they do this by 'fanning' it with their tails.

Notes: They can hold their breath under water for five or six minutes. Their nostrils close automatically when the head is under water. Body produces red-coloured liquid to keep skin moist.

Status: Locally common.

Food: Grazer^G; feeds mostly on grass and small plants on or near riverbanks and lagoons.

Reproduction: Mates in the water; single calf weighing 30kg born after eight-month gestation^G period.

Giraffe

Giraffa camelopardalis

African names: Kameelperd (A); indlulamthi, (X); indlulamithi (Z).

Average size: Height 4.5m (m), 4m (f); weight 1,200kg (m), 900kg (f).

Identification: Tall; long, thin legs and long, sturdy neck. Coat covered with mottled brown patches. Sharp, pointed face; two horn-like knobs (covered with skin) on the head.

Where found: Thornveld.

Habits: Lives in groups of up to 20; most active in early morning and late afternoon.

Notes: Makes snorting sounds. It is the tallest land mammal.

Status: Locally common.

Food: Browser^G; spends most of the day eating from high branches. Curls its lips and 45cm tongue around twigs and pulls off leaves. Favours acacia trees.

Reproduction: 15-month gestation^G; single calf of 100kg.

Blue Wildebeest

Connochaetes taurinus

African names: Blouwildebees (A); inyamakazi eluhlaza yasehlathini (X); indonkoni eluhlaza (Z).

Average size: Height 1.5m (m), 1.3m (f); weight 250kg (m), 180kg (f).

Identification: Dark grey body, with broad chest and wide shoulders. Stripe-like marks running down from neck to chest. Broad face with hair hanging from the throat; pair of curved horns; long-haired tail.

Where found: Open savanna and plains covered with grass.

Habits: Gregarious[G]. Usually herds of up to 30, but sometimes thousands when migrating[G]. Bulls are strictly territorial[G].

Notes: Calves can walk almost immediately after they are born. Its horns are not as curved as black wildebeest's.

Status: Common.

Food: Grazes[G] on short grasses.

Reproduction: Eight-month gestation[G]; single calf weighing 20kg.

Similar species: Black Wildebeest.

Springbok

Antidorcas marsupialis

African names: Springbok (A); ibhadi (X); insephe (Z).

Average size: Height 75cm; weight 40kg.

Identification: Small body; light brown back, white belly, and broad, dark red-brown stripe on the sides. Thin, strong legs, and long, pointed ears. Both ram and ewe have curved, ridged horns, but the male's horns are thicker. Tiny tail.

Where found: Dry, open areas with little vegetation.

Habits: Usually form small herds, but may come together in thousands, especially during migration^G.

Notes: When frightened, the springbok 'pronks', leaping straight-legged into the air with its back arched; it can jump 2m high while doing this.

Status: Common.

Food: Largely a grazer^G, but may also browse^G.

Reproduction: Five-and-a-half-month gestation^G; single lamb weighing 3.5kg.

African Buffalo

Syncerus caffer

African names: Buffel (A); inyathi (X, Z).

Average size: Height 1.4m; weight 700kg.

Identification: Sturdy, dark brown body; wide, strong back; short legs and large hooves. Ears are long and hang below the face. Tuft of dark hair on tip of tail. Males and females have massive, curved horns. Hair sparse in old bulls.

Where found: Prefers woodland savanna.

Habits: Gregarious[G]; lives in large herds, often numbering hundreds of animals – males, females and their young. Some bulls may form small bachelor[G] herds.

Notes: Although both cows and bulls have big horns, the bull usually has a much heavier 'boss', or hard (cap-like base of the horn).

Status: Locally common.

Food: Grazer[G].

Reproduction: 11-month gestation[G]; a single calf weighing 40kg.

Greater Kudu

Tragelaphus strepsiceros

African names: Koedoe (A); iqhudu (X); umgankla (Z).

Average size: Height 1.5m; weight 250kg (m), 180kg (f).

Identification: Light brown body, with pale stripes running down each side. Large, leaf-shaped ears, and a bushy tail. The bull has impressive spiral horns.

Where found: Lives in savanna woodland areas, and even in dry, rocky landscapes.

Habits: Cows and calves form herds of about four to 10, while bulls live either on their own or in bachelor^G herds. Diurnal^G.

Notes: An excellent jumper, it can clear a fence of over 2m!

Status: Common.

Food: Browser^G; eats the leaves of an enormous variety of different bushes and low trees – more than that of any other antelope in southern Africa.

Reproduction: Seven-month gestation^G period; gives birth to a single calf weighing 15kg.

Common Dolphin

Delphinus

African names: Kortsnoet-gewone dolfyn, langsnoet-gewone dolfyn (A); ihlengesi eliqhelekileyo (X); ihlengethwa elivamile (Z).

Average size: Length 2.5m; weight 150kg.

Identification: Dark grey back, with grey and mustard-coloured shapes on the sides; dark stripe from around the eyes down into the elongated, pointed beak. Sharp, curved dorsal fin; long, tapered pectoral fins.

Where found: Shallow and deep, warm pelagic (sea) waters throughout the region.

Habits: Commonly found in groups of about 20. Dives underwater for only short periods. Jumps out of the water when chasing flying fish.

Notes: Curved crisscross pattern along its sides.

Food: Small fish, such as anchovies and sardines, and squid.

Reproduction: 11-month gestation^G; single calf is 1m long and weighs 40kg.

Status: Common offshore.

Similar species: Bottlenose Dolphin.

Southern Right Whale

Eubalaena australis

African names: Suidelike noordkaper (A); umkhoma (X); umnenga wasekunene waseMazantsi (Z).

Average size: Length 17m; weight 6,000kg.

Identification: Very large, dark grey body, with heavy front, tapering towards the large, pointed flukes (at end of tail). Pectoral fins shaped like a paddle; no dorsal fin. Whale lice and barnacles settle on areas of thick skin (callosites) on head – making them white.

Where found: Migrates[G] between waters of the Antarctic (November to April), and oceans north and south of the tropics (May to October).

Habits: Swims slowly. Whales 'breach', or push their bodies backwards out of the sea, then crash back down into the water.

Notes: Called southern 'right' whale; it was considered by early whalers as the 'right' whale to hunt, because it floats when dead.

Status: Seasonally common.

Food: Specialist feeder on copepods[G].

Reproduction: 12-month gestation[G]; single calf measuring 6m.

Glossary

Abdomen: Back part of spider's body, behind head and thorax.

Arboreal: Living in trees.

Bachelor: Non-breeding male.

Browser: An animal that feeds on leaves and fruits of trees and bushes.

Carapace: The hard shield covering the top of the fused head and thorax of a spider; also the upper section of tortoise or turtle shell.

Copepods: One of the small organisms that make up plankton.

Diagnostic: A feature that conclusively identifies an animal.

Diurnal: Active during the day.

Endemic: Occurring only in a particular region.

Gestation: Pregnancy; time during which developing young is carried in the womb of the mother.

Grazer: An animal that feeds mostly on grass and ground-covering plants.

Gregarious: Social, living in groups or colonies.

Incubation: Regulate egg temperature; period of time eggs take to hatch.

IUCN Red (Data) List: International list of threatened or endangered species.

Juvenile: Young bird or animal.

Migratory: Moving from one region to another, with the seasons.

Monogamous: Having only one mate during a breeding season.

Neurotoxin: Poison that interferes with the electrical activity of the nerves.

Nocturnal: Active at night.

Omnivorous: Eating any type of food.

Predator: An animal that hunts and feeds on other animals.

Spinnerets: The abdominal appendages through which the silk is produced.

Terrestrial: Living on the ground.

Territorial: Staying in a marked off area, defended against others.

Photographic Credits

Adrian Bailey: pg 40; **Andrew Bannister:** pg 47 (IOA); **Michael Brett:** pg 5; **Tony Camacho:** pg 1 (right), 23, 29; **Roger de la Harpe/IOA:** pg 16; **Nigel J. Dennis:** front cover (deep etch), back cover (bottom), pg 15, 27, 35 (IOA), 37 (IOA), 38 (IOA), 41, 43, 45, 46, 51 (IOA), 53; **Albert Froneman:** pg 26, 30, 31, 34; **R Haestier:** pg 54; **S C Hendricks:** pg 33; **Lex Hes:** front cover (left & top right), pg 2, 6, 17, 21, 22, 24, 32, 39, 48, 52; **Leonard Hoffman/IOA:** front cover (bottom), pg 13, 14; **N Larson:** pg 10, 11, 12, back cover (top), pg 4; **Gerry Nelson:** pg 8; **Peter Pickford:** pg 28 (IOA), 42, 50, 55; **A Pouw:** pg 3 (left), 18, 19; **Austin J Stevens:** pg 4, 36, 49; **Erhardt Thiel:** pg 44 (IOA); **David Thorpe/IOA:** pg 55; **Lanz van Horsten:** pg 3 (right) (IOA), 9 (IOA); **John Visser:** pg 1 (left), 20; **R Vos:** pg 25.

IOA = Images of Africa

The author, Sean Fraser, acknowledges the entries in Birds, Reptiles and Arthropods contributed by Tracey Hawthorne.